BASTILLE
D0841649
LA CONCIERGERIE
THE FRENCH
REVOLUTION
PALAIS DES TUILERIES

THE FRENCH REVOLUTION

ODYSSEYS

KATE RIGGS

CREATIVE EDUCATION • CREATIVE PAPERBACKS

Published by Creative Education and Creative Paperbacks
P.O. Box 227, Mankato, Minnesota 56002
Creative Education and Creative Paperbacks
are imprints of The Creative Company
www.thecreativecompany.us

Design and production by Blue Design
Art direction by Rita Marshall
Printed in the United States of America

Photographs by The Bridgeman Art Library (Giraudon), Corbis (Bass Museum of Art, Bettmann, Stefano Bianchetti, Gianni Dagli Orti, Historical Picture Archive, Leemage, Francis G. Mayer, Philippe Renault/Hemis, The Art Archive), Getty Images (After Maurice Quentin de la Tour, Bridgeman Art Library, Alexandre Evariste Fragonard, French School, George Hamilton, Victor-Henri Juglar, Louis Leopold Boilly, Jean Pierre Franque, Charles Marie Rigobert Bonne, Philibert Rouviere)

Library of Congress Cataloging-in-Publication Data
Riggs, Kate.
The French Revolution / Kate Riggs.
p. cm. — (Odysseys in history)
Summary: A look at the causes and global effects of the 1789 storming of the Bastille and subsequent decade-long revolution, which toppled a monarchy but paved the way for Napoleon's rise to power.
Includes bibliographical references and index.
ISBN 978-1-60818-526-9 (hardcover)
ISBN 978-1-62832-127-2 (pbk)
1. France—History—Revolution, 1789-1799—Juvenile literature. I. Title.

DC148.R54 2015
944.04—dc23 2014041764

CCSS: RI.8.1, 2, 3, 4; RI.9-10.1, 2, 3, 4; RI.11-12.1, 2, 3, 4; RH.6-8.1, 4, 5, 7; RH.9-10.1, 3, 4

First Edition HC 9 8 7 6 5 4 3 2 1
First Edition PBK 9 8 7 6 5 4 3 2 1

Cover: *Storming of the Bastille*, by Jean-Pierre Houël
Page 2: The July Revolution of 1830
Pages 4–5: *View of the Orangerie, the Hundred Steps, and the Chateau at Versailles*, by Jean-Baptiste Martin
Page 6: French Revolutionary battle

CONTENTS

Introduction

As heavy clouds loomed over the city of Paris, France, a restless crowd gathered. At almost 1,000 strong, it overwhelmed the area outside the walls of the royal prison known as the Bastille. It was early in the morning of July 14, 1789. The people of Paris were beginning to panic. They had seen the soldiers stationed outside the city and began to fear that their untrustworthy king had planned an

OPPOSITE: The leisurely activities enjoyed by some of France's middle class were interrupted by the Revolution's goals of providing freedom, equality, and brotherhood to all.

attack against them. Approaching the keeper of the Bastille, the band of citizens demanded that he release the ammunition and guns stored there, so that they might better protect themselves. The keeper refused, but the Parisians would not take no for an answer. They attacked the fortress and took the case for liberty into their own hands.

In storming the Bastille, the people of Paris began a new age. It was an age of revolution and civil disobedience. It was an age that would topple a monarchy but make way for an emperor. Yet on the night of July 14, all that the people could see was the symbol of royal power that had been destroyed before their eyes. Throughout the streets of Paris, the triumphant shout was heard, "The Bastille has fallen, its gates are open!"

July 14, 1789

Change Is in the Air

There are many theories about how the French Revolution started. The most popular theory holds that it began with the bourgeoisie, or France's middle class, who were discontentedly living by the rules set up for them by the higher class of nobles. Later, some historians proposed that it was the backlash of the peasants against the economic crisis of the time that brought the French Revolution to its final and most desperate form. But no matter which class was to blame, all classes shared a growing dislike for and frustration with one thing: the monarchy.

French kings had ruled as absolute monarchs—unchecked by a lawmaking body such as a congress or parliament—since the Middle Ages. Such power had become a heavy responsibility to bear by 1789. Unable to live up to the sparkling reign of Louis XIV, "The Sun King," whose rule ended in 1715, later kings distanced themselves from the people and ignored many problems, such as the government's increasing debt and its unequal system of taxation.

Louis XVI, France's king from 1774 until 1789, wanted to be a popular and kindly king, but he did not know how to do it. He was plagued by self-doubt and relied heavily on his advisers (and often his queen, Marie-Antoinette) to make important political decisions for him. Despite what he witnessed happening around the world, such as the conflict between Great Britain and the American colonies, he saw no need to radically change France's course to reflect the changing times. This lack of vision would eventually cost him his throne—and his life.

Unlike the government, the Catholic Church in France was a well-oiled machine prior to the Revolution. It operated above many laws that applied to common

OPPOSITE When Louis XVI assumed the throne of France in May 1774, he was almost 20 years old and had led a sheltered life as a well-educated aristocrat with no practical life experience.

people. For example, priests and other members of the clergy did not have to pay taxes. In addition, the Church owned about a tenth of the land in France and became wealthy by charging other people to rent it. Because the Church was powerful in so many ways, it could have been a major threat to the monarchy. Yet it rarely complained against the king's policies.

Other organizations did complain, though. Courts of law known as *parlements*, which represented the 13 districts into which France was divided, often voiced and acted upon their opposition. Parlements could ignore national laws if they disagreed with them, fixing prices on goods, censoring books, and outlawing whatever they thought was inappropriate. The magistrates, or heads, of the parlements got away with such behavior because they owned their positions for as long as they wanted them—they

Marie-Antoinette

Queen Marie-Antoinette was infamous for her lavish tastes, ignorance of the plight of the French people, and general disdain for the Revolution, but many credit her as the true mind behind the monarchy. Married to Louis XVI when she was 15 and forced to leave her home country of Austria, Marie-Antoinette felt like a lonely outsider at the French royal court for several years until Louis became king in 1774. More decisive than her husband and prone to secretly negotiate with anyone who could help the royal family, Marie-Antoinette kept the monarchy intact—but fueled the public's hatred of the couple—until 1792.

paid the government to serve as magistrates. It was usually impossible for the government to remove magistrates from their posts because it then had to refund their money.

Such a disjointed approach to governing began to frustrate the masses. France, along with the rest of Europe, was in the midst of the Age of Enlightenment, a time during the 1700s when reason, science, and humanitarian ideas were valued and talked about. Notable thinkers such as Frenchmen Jean-Jacques Rousseau and Voltaire and English-American Thomas Paine influenced

"It is seldom acknowledged now how far [the Terror] was (much like the American Revolution) a civil war, deriving much of its grim impetus [momentum] from the inevitable bitterness of conflict between former friends. Seldom, too, is it recognized just how important and active a role the enemies of the Revolution played in the aggravation of its politics—how eagerly, for example, the king and queen of France steered the country into foreign war, with the avowed intention of using the conflict to destroy the Revolution."

David Andress, historian, 2005

BELOW The French admired the landmark actions taken by American revolutionaries such as the signing of the Declaration of Independence on July 4, 1776, in Philadelphia, Pennsylvania.

the discussions and literature of people throughout the Western world (the part of the world including Europe and America). Enlightened people wanted to have a say in their government. In response, some officials in King Louis XVI's administration tried to experiment with new ways of governing, suggesting such reforms as making the nobles pay taxes. These attempts at reform were at first unsuccessful in France, but elsewhere, efforts to break from tradition won out.

The French watched with great interest as their friends in the American British colonies fought a war for independence and won. The American Revolution, which lasted from 1775 to 1783, inspired like-minded people in France. They realized that they did not have to sit by while their government fell apart and made unreasonable decisions. They saw that the Enlightenment's ideals of self-government, knowledge, and reason could be effectively put into practice. By the time the Americans were fighting for their liberty, the French had become convinced that a fresh start was possible for them, too.

Throughout the 1700s, the philosophies of the Enlightenment had taken root and produced more educated readers in France than ever before. For the nobles and bourgeoisie who knew how to read, who owned property, and who had time to improve their minds, the Age of Enlightenment provided the perfect opportunity to come together and discuss common issues. The upsurge in the production of weekly and daily newspapers and books, along with improved accessibility to reading rooms and public libraries, gave people more resources than ever before to turn to for information.

However, not all of France was swept away by the Enlightenment. People who lived outside of Paris and other major cities likely did not hear about such theories until much later in the century. The movement, though, became a central theme in the argument used by people who thought that France's government needed to change. Eventually, such critics convinced their fellow citizens that the monarchy was corrupt and intolerable. They called into question Louis XVI's ability to rule and a royal court that lived as extravagantly as Louis and Marie-Antoinette did. Once people lost faith in the government and began to see that Louis was irresponsible with money, individual investors and foreign countries stopped loaning money to the French. Without loans and because the country did not generate enough money from taxes, the government's funding ran out. It did not help matters that the French government had also recently loaned other countries—such as the fledgling United States—large sums of money, and those loans had not yet been repaid.

From August 1788 until May 1789, the French government was at a standstill. Without funding, it simply was not able to operate. In May 1789, Louis XVI was forced to convene a representative assembly called the Estates-General. (Consisting of members of the Catholic clergy, the nobles, and the bourgeoisie, the Estates-General comprised representatives from the three recognized estates, or classes, in French society. The poorest citizens,

Patriotic Colors

Red, white, and blue are familiar and symbolic colors to Americans, but they were also representative of the French Revolution and, later, the French republic. The signature colors of Paris—blue and red—combined with the symbol of royalty, white, to form the tricolor cockade, or three-colored bow of ribbons. Any citizen who was a true patriot of the Revolution proudly displayed the tricolor cockade on his or her hat or embellished some other article of clothing with it. The cockade lives on today in the flag of modern France: three equal, vertical bands of blue, white, and red.

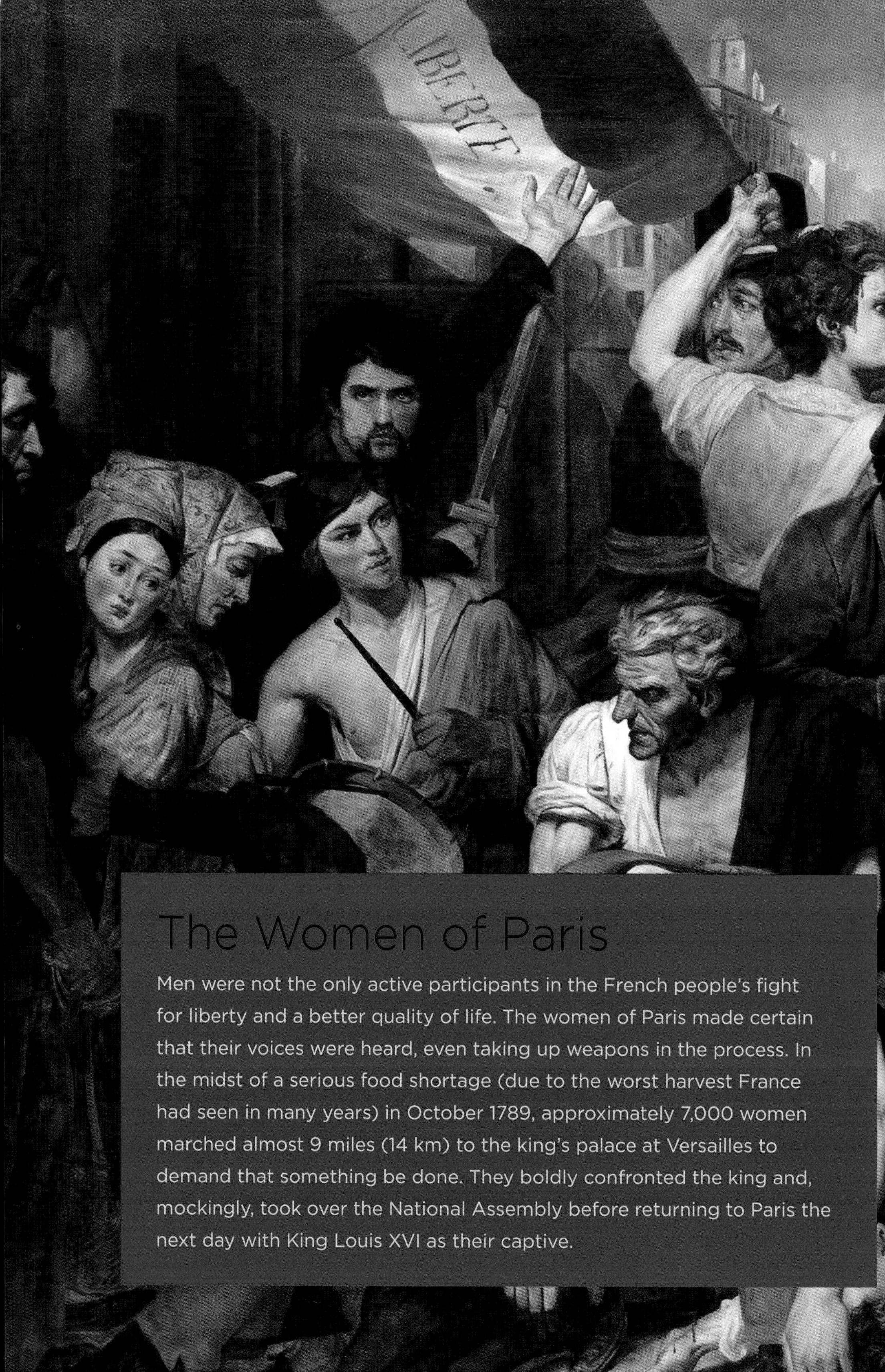

The Women of Paris

Men were not the only active participants in the French people's fight for liberty and a better quality of life. The women of Paris made certain that their voices were heard, even taking up weapons in the process. In the midst of a serious food shortage (due to the worst harvest France had seen in many years) in October 1789, approximately 7,000 women marched almost 9 miles (14 km) to the king's palace at Versailles to demand that something be done. They boldly confronted the king and, mockingly, took over the National Assembly before returning to Paris the next day with King Louis XVI as their captive.

the peasants, went unrepresented.) When this meeting was announced, it signaled to the people that the king was no longer in control of his own country. Citizens in the capital city of Paris began to get anxious.

Eighteenth-century France was dominated by nobles in every part of society, from the royalty down through government, law, business, military, and the Church. Although they had the greatest amount of wealth, power, and influence, nobles were the smallest class, making up between 0.5 and 1.5 percent of the population. At the time of the French Revolution, in 1789, it was easiest to see the great differences between the rich nobles and the poor working class in the capital city of Paris, where all classes were represented. The city's population had reached about 600,000 by then, and its overwhelming majority of working-class citizens were against the king and for a radical change in government.

Paris was also a place that attracted migrant workers, or people who moved about according to where jobs were available. At the time of the Revolution, a large number of migrants settled in the city because they could not find work in the country, where crop harvests were poor and many people were struggling to survive already. The police mistrusted the migrants, blaming public unrest on people who were desperate to do anything for food or money. But what authorities should have feared were the established Parisians of the middle class who lived and worked together in organized communities and owned property. These were the ordinary people who knew their government had let them down and were starting to prepare themselves to fight for something different. With the monarchy deflated, it was only a matter of time before a new system took its place, and by the summer of 1789, that regime was called revolution.

Blood in the Streets

When the Estates-General gathered in May 1789, the meeting did not go as Louis XVI and his officials had planned. For the first month, the three estates could not even agree on how to conduct the meetings, let alone on how to solve the economic problems that faced their country. The rest of France sensed weakness on the part of the king, who was supossed to be

OPPOSITE: The storming of the Bastille on July 14, 1789, marked a turning point in the French Revolution as a symbolic victory against the monarchy.

in charge of the representatives.

On June 10, the third estate, made up of the bourgeoisie, voted rebelliously to proceed without the delegates from the first two estates. Representing 95 percent of the French population, the bourgeoisie delegates felt they had a responsibility to their fellow citizens to take matters into their own hands. Renaming themselves the National Constituent Assembly, the bourgeoisie were able to convince most of the clergy to side with them eventually, and by August, the Assembly would be on its way toward full—though forced—cooperation among the estates.

But before the National Assembly could produce a new plan for the country, revolutionary passion erupted in Paris in early July. For three months, citizens had been staging protests and marching in the streets against a government they felt was ineffective and unfair. When French and foreign troops began surrounding the city in July 1789, their fears of a military backlash seemed to be coming true. Louis XVI had many relatives and supporters in such countries as the German kingdom of Prussia and in Austria, and he did not hesitate to call on them for support and protection.

To prepare themselves in case the soldiers attacked, Parisians began raiding government-owned stores of guns and ammunition. In the two days leading up to the famous storming of the Bastille, citizens also opened the federal prisons to release people who would fight with them. After mobs looted the military barracks of Les Invalides on July 13 and came away with weapons but no ammunition, they realized they needed the gunpowder that was stored at the Bastille on the other side of the city.

"We passed over the main drawbridge, which was raised; I took off my hat and shouted with all my might that the City had sent a deputation to parley [discuss the situation], that they must all cease fire and lay down their arms. A person in a colored coat, in the midst of a group of pensioners [soldiers] ... answered me from the summit of the citadel that he was willing to receive the deputation, but that the crowd must withdraw."

Boucheron, member of the delegation appointed to speak with the keeper of the Bastille, July 14, 1789

The Bastille was an eight-towered fortress that had been built between 1356 and 1382 at the eastern entrance of Paris. From the mid-1460s until 1789, it functioned as a prison. Most importantly, though, it was a prison under the king's direct control, and as such, it was a symbol of the type of absolute power that Parisians had come to resent.

Members of the Mob

The mobs that attacked the Bastille and marched bloodily through the streets of Paris on July 14, 1789, were made up of Parisians from all quarters and professions. They were young children (a boy of eight was one of the first to scale the towers of the Bastille), old men in their 70s, and every age in between. Most were artisans, or craftspeople, such as furniture makers and cobblers, and others were merchants, members of the bourgeoisie, and soldiers. In June 1790, the National Assembly awarded 954 people a special honor for their part in taking the Bastille.

At 9:00 A.M. on July 14, a delegation was sent into the Bastille to negotiate with the director of the prison for gunpowder and the release of its seven prisoners. After waiting for an hour for the delegation to return, the crowd outside became agitated and attacked the small force of veteran French soldiers and their backup of Swiss guards. To get inside the Bastille, many people scaled the walls and towers, while others barged through the front gates.

Once the Bastille fell, Parisians became thirsty for more bloodshed and vengeance. They wanted anyone who was responsible for denying them their demands for arms and freedom to pay. Many public officials—including the keeper of the Bastille, the Marquis de Launay, and the mayor of Paris, Jacques de Flesselles—lost their lives that day. Those who were beaten and killed by citizen mobs served as examples of how far the people would go to provoke radical change in their country.

"While sitting here a person comes in and announces the taking of the Bastille, the governor of which is beheaded and the Prevost des Marchands [Provost of the Merchants, or mayor, Jacques de Flesselles] is killed and also beheaded; they are carrying the heads in triumph through the city. The carrying [capture] of this citadel is among the most extraordinary things that I have met with; it cost the assailants sixty men, it is said."

Gouverneur Morris, American diplomat in Paris, July 14, 1789

While Parisians were gathering arms, peasants also revolted against their lords. France still followed the medieval practice of feudalism, in which poor farmers

OPPOSITE Louis XVI and Marie-Antoinette tried to protect their two remaining children (the other two had died at young ages by October 1789) from the frightening times of the Revolution.

and laborers worked for men called lords but were not allowed to own property. To prevent all-out rebellion, the National Assembly outlawed feudalism on August 4, 1789. Twenty-two days later, the Assembly introduced the Declaration of the Rights of Man and of the Citizen. Like the Americans' Declaration of Independence, the Declaration of the Rights of Man outlined the rights each citizen would have under a new government: liberty, equality, property, and the right to resist oppression.

"Scorn the suggestions and the lies of your false friends; return to your king; he will always be your father, your best friend. What pleasure he will have in forgetting all his personal insults, and in seeing himself again amongst you."

Louis XVI, King of France, addressing his subjects in a letter he left behind when he fled Paris in 1791

OPPOSITE *Bastille* is a French word that means "castle" or "stronghold," and the four-story prison building, complete with eight towers and surrounded by a moat, lived up to the name.

King Louis refused to affirm the Assembly's actions, but his voice was drowned out quickly by the demands of the revolutionaries. Although the king continued to play a role in the new government, he could now be outvoted.

The majority of the French population embraced the new system that put elected representatives of the people in charge in the fall of 1789. They joined political clubs (or branches of clubs) such as the Jacobins and the Cordeliers. They also held public ceremonies that celebrated the spirit of the Revolution such as by planting cypress trees, which were called "trees of liberty." On July 14, 1790, French citizens gathered in Paris on the first anniversary of the storming of the Bastille for the Festival of Federation. They ate together at long tables set up on a field called the Champ de Mars and toasted their (supposedly) unified country.

"I dreamed of a republic that all the world would love! I could never have believed that men were so ferocious and so unjust! ... And considering that our colleagues [other Montagnards] are so cowardly to abandon us and to bend their ears to these calumnies [slanderous words] that I cannot understand, but which are surely the most grotesque possible, I see now that we die victims of our own courageous denunciation of traitors and our love of the truth!"

Camille Desmoulins, influential Revolutionary journalist and victim of the Terror, 1794

Those who had opposed the Revolution from the beginning were not sympathetic to its progress. Known as *émigrés*, or "the emigrated," they were nobles who had left France in 1789 and moved to neighboring countries such as Spain and Austria. From there, they secretly

Festival of Federation

The first anniversary of the storming of the Bastille was celebrated with the Festival of Federation, a communal, open-air meal and party held on the Champ de Mars field in Paris and elsewhere throughout the country on July 14, 1790. The Festival symbolized the unification of the country and how the citizens could act as one entity, or body, now that they were free from the absolute rule of a monarch. It also represented how the new nation did not need the king it still had; Louis XVI stood on the outskirts of the celebration, present but largely ignored.

worked with Louis and Marie-Antoinette to gain foreign support to help Louis take back his country. This force became known as the counter-revolution. After Louis refused to cooperate with the National Assembly in jointly ruling the country and tried to escape France, the royal family became prisoners in their Paris palace in 1791. By early 1792, their only hope was to cause a war that might bring foreign armies to rescue them.

"I was a queen, and you took away my crown, a wife, and you killed my husband, a mother, and you took my children away from me. All I have left is my blood. Take it. But do not make me suffer long."

Marie-Antoinette, Queen of France, before she was beheaded in 1793

Both the king and the most radical leaders of the National Assembly decided to declare war on Austria, a powerful empire at the time, in April 1792. Austria's army at first outnumbered the French, and France suffered many defeats, leaving the French feeling betrayed—again—by the king who had led them into war. (It was not until the following year that the French army would strengthen its forces with about 500,000 new recruits and not until 1802 that this stage of the fighting would end.) On September 20, 1792, the National Assembly, now called the National Convention, met. In two days' time, it did away with the monarchy and declared France a republic, a government controlled solely by the people and their elected representatives.

"The path leading to the scaffold was extremely rough and difficult to pass; the King was obliged to lean on my arm, and from the slowness with which he proceeded, I feared for a moment that his courage might fail; but what was my astonishment, when arrived at the last step, I felt that he suddenly let go my arm, and I saw him cross with a firm foot the breadth of the whole scaffold."

Henry Edgeworth, English priest who accompanied Louis XVI to the guillotines in 1793

The National Convention was split into two camps: the Girondins and the Montagnards. The Girondins wanted to carry the bourgeois-led Revolution into the rest of Europe, freeing other countries from their monarchies as well. The Montagnards, headed by extremist lawyer Maximilien Robespierre, wanted to continue the Revolution in France instead and give more political power

The September Massacres

An event called the September Massacres is sometimes also known as the "First Terror" of the Revolution's Reign of Terror period. After the royal family was imprisoned by revolutionary mobs in their Parisian palace in August 1792, many citizens became paranoid that Paris's political prisoners (who were jailed because they were accused of being enemies of the Revolution) were plotting to break out of the prisons to join the counter-revolutionary forces that supported the king. From September 2 to September 6, about 1,200 prisoners were killed in a surge of irrational violence that horrified nations around the world.

to the lower classes. Although the two sides agreed that the monarchy should end, the Montagnards favored a more brutal way of achieving it: they overpowered the Girondins in deciding to put Louis and Marie-Antoinette to death for treason in 1793.

The Montagnards received the most support from a group of Parisian workers, craftsmen, and shopkeepers called the *sans-culottes*. Under pressure from them, the Montagnards instituted several new programs, including government control of prices, taxation of the rich, and free education. They also authorized the sales of the properties of émigrés. When the war abroad against Austria, Prussia, and their allies began to sour again in the spring of 1793, the Montagnards were able to take over the government on a campaign platform of change.

To increase reform, Robespierre and the Montagnards decided to punish anyone who was viewed as an enemy of the Revolution. This period of vengeance against political rivals, the Catholic Church, and nobles was called the Reign of Terror, and it lasted from September 5, 1793, to July 27, 1794. Of the 300,000 people arrested as "suspects" during the Terror, 17,000 were sentenced to death and executed, and many more were left to die in prison or killed without trial. Such extreme measures would land Robespierre himself on the executioner's platform on July 28, 1794, when both his life and the Reign of Terror came to an end.

MANCHE
Pas de Calais
FLANDRE
ARTOIS
HAINAUT
LILLE
AMIENS
GÉN. D'AMIENS
GÉN. DE ROUEN
GÉNÉRALITÉ DE PARIS
Gᵀᴱ DE SOISSONS
GÉNÉRA. DE CHALONS
LORRAINE
GÉN. DE CAEN
GÉN. D'ALENÇON
GÉNÉRALITÉ DE TOURS
GÉNER. D'ORLÉANS
GÉN. DE BOURGES
GÉNÉRALITÉ DE MOULINS
GÉNÉRALITÉ DE DIJON
FRANCHE-COMTÉ
GÉNÉRALITÉ DE POITIERS
Gᵀᴱ DE LA ROCHELLE
GÉN. DE LIMOGES
GÉNÉRALITÉ DE RIOM
GÉN. DE LYON
GÉNER. DE RIOM
GÉN. DE BORDEAUX
Gᴱ DE MONTAUBAN
GÉN. DE MONTPELLIER
Gᵀᴱ DE GRENOBLE
GÉNÉRALITÉ D'AUCH
Gᴱ DE BAYONNE
GÉN. DE PAU
GÉN. DE TOULOUSE
ROUSSILLON
Monts Pyrenees
GOLFE DE LION
MER
Dunkerque
Calais
Boulogne
S. Omer
Ypres
Arras
Abbeville
Cambray
Valenciennes
Mons
Namur
Charlemont
Givet
S. Valery
Dieppe
Fecamp
le Havre
ROUEN
Cherbourg
Bayeux
CAEN
Coutances
Avranches
Lizieux
Evreux
Beauvais
Soissons
Laon
Reims
Rethel
Sedan
Luxembourg
Thionville
Metz
Verdun
Toul
Nancy
Pontoise
S. Germain
Versailles
PARIS
Meaux
CHAALONS
Provins
Sezane
Vitry le François
Joinville
Melun
Fontainebleau
Sens
Troyes
Bar sur Aube
Chartres
Dourdan
ALENÇON
Mortagne
Rennes
Mayenne
le Mans
Laval
la Fleche
Vendômes
Chau Dun
ORLEANS
Blois
Montargis
Auxerre
Joigny
Tonnerre
Chatillon
Langres
Dijon
Nuits
Beaune
Dole
Salins
Besançon
Gray
Pontarlier
Semur
Vezelay
Briare
Cosne
la Charite
Nevers
Angers
TOURS
NANTES
Saumur
Chinon
Amboise
Loches
Romorentin
Henrichemont
BOURGES
Issoudun
Chateau Roux
le Blanc
Bourbon l'Archambaut
MOULINS
Autun
Arnay le Duc
Challon
Charolles
Macon
Bourg
Lons le Saunier
S. Claude
Ville Franche
Trevoux
LYON
Belley
Vienne
GRENOBLE
Valence
Die
Gap
Fontevraut
Mauleon
Luçon
Fontenai le Cte
POITIERS
LA ROCHELLE
I. de Ré
I. d'Oleron
T. de Cordouan
Saintes
Angouleme
le Dorat
Gueret
LIMOGES
Montluçon
Vichy
RIOM
Clermont
Montbrison
Perigueux
Tulle
Brives
Aurillac
S. Flour
le Puy
BORDEAUX
Sarlat
Cahors
Mende
Viviers
Bazas
Clerac
Agen
V. Franche
Rhodez
Milhaud
Condom
MONTAUBAN
Lectoure
AUCH
Alby
Lavaur
Vabre
Lodeve
Alais
Uzes
Orange
Avignon
Carpentras
Nismes
Arles
MONTPELLIER
Aix
Marseille
Toulon
Bayonne
S. Sever
Acqs
Aire
Mirande
Tarbe
Bagneres
TOULOUSE
Castres
S. Pons
S. Papoul
Rieux
Mirepoix
Carcassonne
Narbonne
Beziers
Agde
Pamiers
Foix
Alet
Perpignan
Mᵗ Louis
Porquerolles

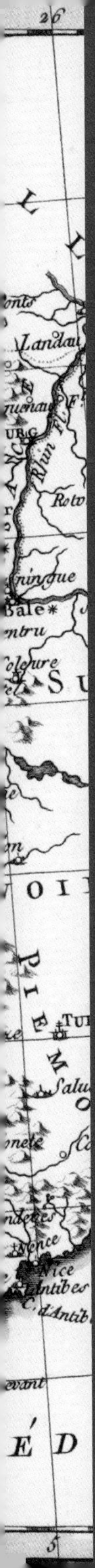

From Equality to Empire

After the disastrous Reign of Terror ended, it was difficult for the Montagnard leaders of the National Convention to gain further support for any other extreme policies. Political power changed hands once again. Disillusioned and hungry because of more food and grain shortages throughout the difficult winter of 1794–95, the people of France began to turn the tide against the radical

OPPOSITE: Guillaume-Thomas Raynal, a French historian popular for his radical political views at the time of the Revolution, created this map showing France's regions around 1780.

element that had driven the Terror. They moved instead toward forming a government that would be committed to expanding the ideals of the Revolution—liberty, equality, property ownership, and freedom from oppression—through war. This was the new government's goal, and it was achieved to some extent, but the remembrance of the horrors of the Terror prevented full revolutions from taking effect in many countries.

"The chief permanent achievement of the French Revolution was the suppression of those political institutions, commonly described as feudal, which for many centuries had held unquestioned sway in most European countries. The Revolution set out to replace them with a new social and political order, at once simple and more uniform, based on the concept of the equality of all men."

Alexis de Tocqueville, French political scientist and historian, 1856

Other Europeans viewed what had happened in France and had no desire to repeat the same possible chain of events in their own countries.

By August 1795, the French Revolution had effectively come to an end, and a new constitution made by the National Convention charged a Directory of five members with control over all of the government's decision-making. (The Directory members were elected by the lawmakers of the legislature, the other arm of the reconstructed government.) However, ongoing fighting

Passionate revolutionaries gave stirring speeches to crowds of people, causing them to rethink their political views and spurring them to action during the French Revolution.

CAFE
DE FOY

(by this time with Britain and Germany) proved too much for the newly organized but poorly administered Directory to handle. Many officials fought to take it over with acts of violence called coups. Only a young army general named Napoleon Bonaparte was ultimately successful in staging a coup. On November 9, 1799, he became France's first consul, or government-appointed leader, and a three-member Consulate replaced the Directory.

The revolutionary system of government may have ended in 1795, but the aftershocks from the changes begun in 1789 rippled throughout the country and Europe for a decade. Many of the men who came to power during the height of the Revolution—such as National Assemblyman Emmanuel Sieyès—continued to shape the policies of post-revolutionary France. As these revolutionary-minded people sought to expand the

Revolution to conquered territories in the Netherlands and northern Italy, they hoped to gain so much influence that they could cause other European countries to abandon monarchies for republican systems of government as well. But Bonaparte and several ambitious politicians realized early on that the French war of expansion was an opportunity to build a new empire. Bonaparte had no intention of allowing that kind of power to slip through his fingers.

"What is a throne?—a bit of wood gilded and covered in velvet. I am the state—I alone am here the representative of the people. Even if I had done wrong, you should not have reproached me in public—people wash their dirty linen at home. France has more need of me than I of France."

Napoleon Bonaparte, French emperor, in a statement to the French Senate, 1814

Bonaparte's military victories in such places as Italy, Malta, and Egypt soon made him a national hero. At a time when most of France's armies were retreating in defeat, Bonaparte became known as the shining example of France's success. His status made it easy for him to persuade everyone that, as a product of the Revolution, he was committed to maintaining a free and equal France. His assurances proved to be empty promises. By the time Bonaparte became Emperor Napoleon I in 1804 (reigning until 1815), he had successfully overpowered the government and the people. The voice of the revolutionaries was swallowed by the power-hungry Bonaparte. With a single leader as the face of the government again, many government officials returned to their secretive, corrupt ways, and

Reason as Religion

The French Revolution took the intellectual ideals of the Enlightenment to a new, extreme level, replacing Catholicism with Reason as the national religion. The process began with taking away the clergy's privileges and making the Church's lands state-owned in 1790. Soon, Christian worship was outlawed, and churches were closed or converted into Temples of Reason. Efforts to wipe Christianity out of France for good were, surprisingly, supported by a population that only a few years before had been 95 percent Catholic. The revolutionaries, though, were as fed up with the Church's influence over their lives as they were with the monarchy's, and both institutions paid a high price.

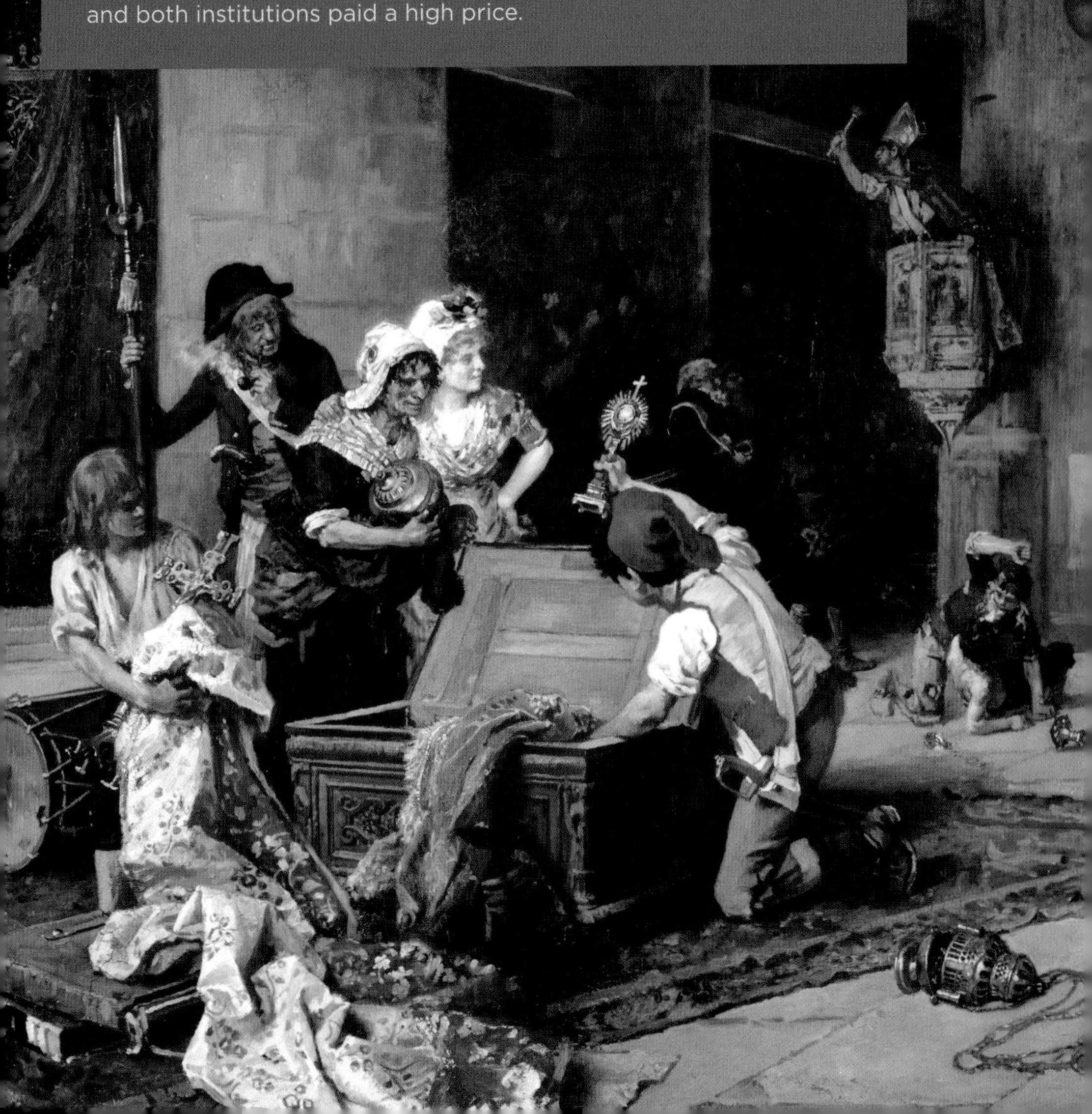

TAKEAWAY

The Revolution had not succeeded in bettering the lives of the poorer people of France.

the Revolution's goals of accountability and fairness seemed to be swept under the rug.

After an intense 10-year period of war—both within the country and outside it—France nevertheless entered the 19th century with confidence. It would need that sense of confidence to face the problems that were lurking just around the corner. The Revolution had not succeeded in bettering the lives of the poorer people of France. Farmers, laborers, and those who lived in rural areas still suffered from a lack of income and were in fact poorer than they had been before the Revolution. Although feudalism had been abandoned, people still found that they had to answer to landlords, and when land formerly held by the Catholic Church was sold by the government, it was the noble class that benefited.

Yet the great majority of citizens (the middle class) who had taken such an interest in politics during the early years of the Revolution did not see the need to continue to struggle against the new government under Bonaparte. By 1799, they found themselves in a changed world. It may not have been the world they had envisioned in 1789, but it was still radically different.

Bonaparte was trained in military schools from the age of nine, and as a young officer in the French army, his displays of heroism on the battlefield were widely celebrated.

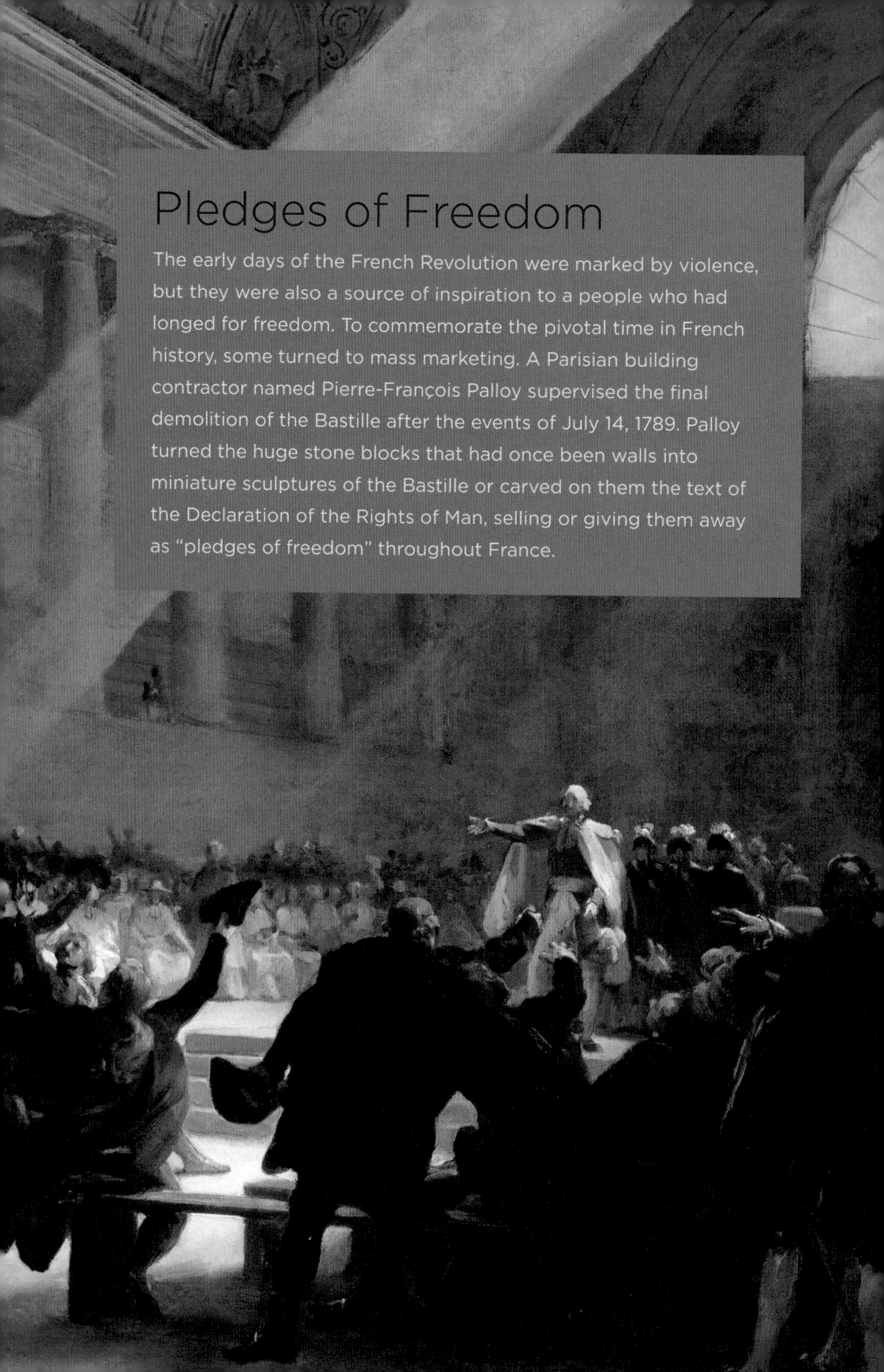

Pledges of Freedom

The early days of the French Revolution were marked by violence, but they were also a source of inspiration to a people who had longed for freedom. To commemorate the pivotal time in French history, some turned to mass marketing. A Parisian building contractor named Pierre-François Palloy supervised the final demolition of the Bastille after the events of July 14, 1789. Palloy turned the huge stone blocks that had once been walls into miniature sculptures of the Bastille or carved on them the text of the Declaration of the Rights of Man, selling or giving them away as "pledges of freedom" throughout France.

France had succeeded in expanding its borders, and food shortages were no longer an everyday concern. Although the economy was (and would continue to be) weak, people did not feel the need to riot against it. The country had experienced trial by fire and had come out stronger and more unified. Because of France's actions, the rest of Europe was also changed—by warfare and idealism—and countries such as the Netherlands and Germany began to take on their modern shapes and boundaries, especially after widespread peace was finally reached throughout Europe by 1802.

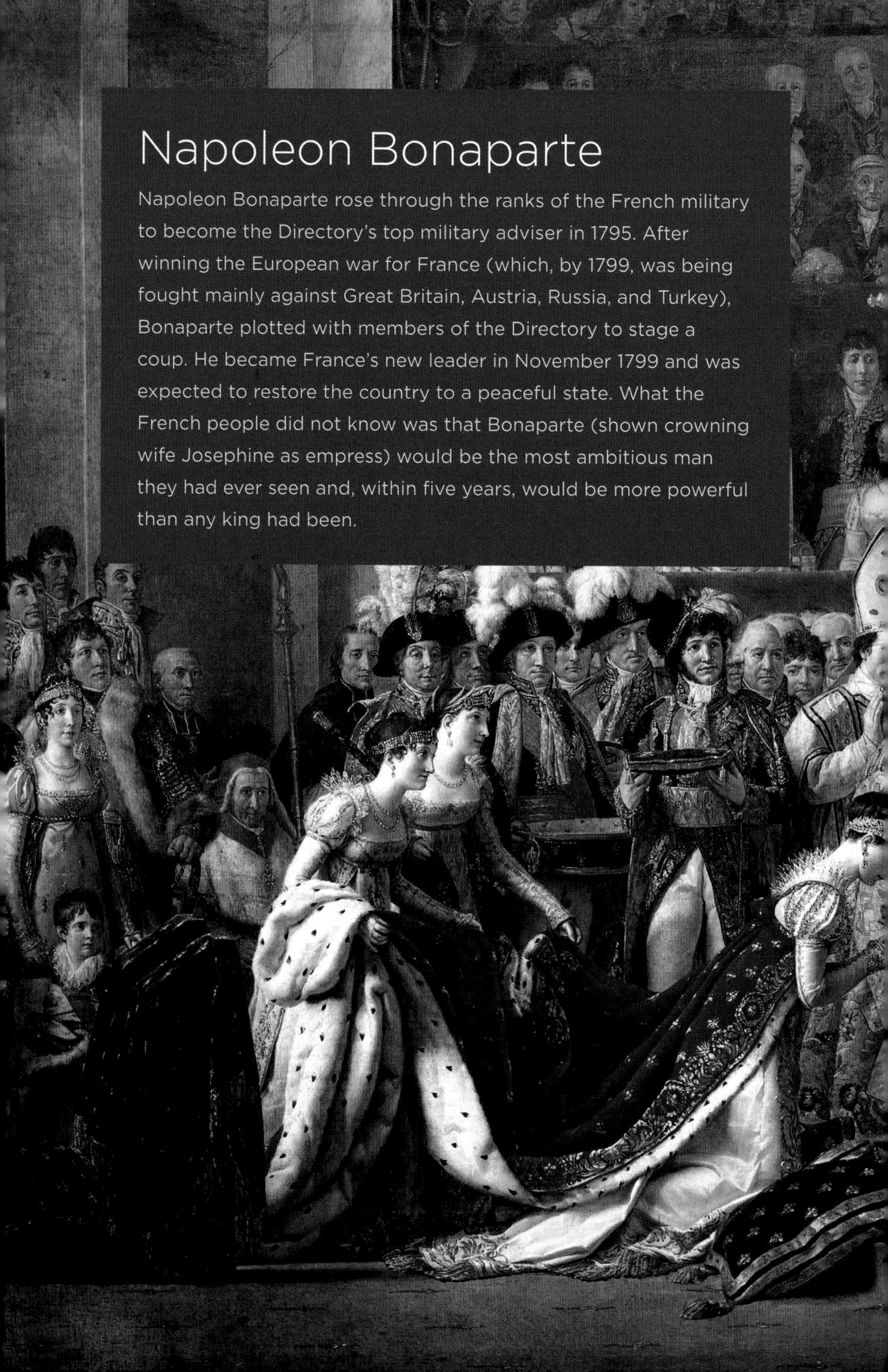

Napoleon Bonaparte

Napoleon Bonaparte rose through the ranks of the French military to become the Directory's top military adviser in 1795. After winning the European war for France (which, by 1799, was being fought mainly against Great Britain, Austria, Russia, and Turkey), Bonaparte plotted with members of the Directory to stage a coup. He became France's new leader in November 1799 and was expected to restore the country to a peaceful state. What the French people did not know was that Bonaparte (shown crowning wife Josephine as empress) would be the most ambitious man they had ever seen and, within five years, would be more powerful than any king had been.

Maintaining that peace was a delicate matter. By 1812, Bonaparte's dreams of empire building began to ignite yet another backlash against the government by a disillusioned public. The France of the 19th century would prove to be highly unstable and unsettled, despite Bonaparte's early reforms in the way laws were made, in his reconciliation of the Catholic Church with the French government, and in his strengthening of the military. After Bonaparte's death in 1821, a new wave of revolutions, including the July Revolution of 1830, began. This produced an alternating succession of republics, monarchies, and short-lived empires until the Fifth Republic was finally established in 1958.

Like any revolution, the French Revolution was imperfect and characterized by more violence than

> Like any revolution, the French Revolution was imperfect and characterized by more violence than was perhaps necessary to change the nation's political structure.

was perhaps necessary to change the nation's political structure. Many revolutionaries felt justified at the time to act in exceedingly violent ways—the mass executions and beheadings of rival political leaders, Catholic priests, and anyone who represented the old order of the monarchy became the most well-known legacy of the Revolution. Yet their reasoning for committing such brutalities in the name of justice and progress did not stand up over time. Even the majority of modern French citizens acknowledge that their revolution was

DÉCLA
DES DROITS
ET DU C
Décretés par l'Assemblée Nationa
23, 24 et 26 aoust 1789,
PRÉAMBULE
LES représantans du peuple Francois, constitués
en assemblée nationale, considérant que l'ignorance,
l'oubli ou le mépris des droits de lhomme sont les seules
causes des malheurs publics et de la corruption des gouvernemens
ont résolu d'exposer dans une déclaration solemnelle, les droits
naturels, inaliénables et sacrés de lhomme: afin que cette décla
ration, constamment présente a tous les membres du corps
social, leur rappelle sans cesse leurs droits et leurs devoirs,
afin que les actes du pouvoir legislatif et ceux du pouvoir ex
cutif, pouvant être a chaque instant comparés avec le but
de toute institution politique, en soient plus respectés; afin que
les reclamations des citoyens, fondées désormais sur des princ
pes simples et incontestables, tournent toujours au maintien
de la constitution et du bonheur de tous.
EN conséquence, l'assemblée nationale reconnoit et déclare,
en presence et sous les auspices de l'Etre suprême les droits

The 17 articles of the Declaration of the Rights of Man and of the Citizen began with a lengthy introductory statement of purpose called a preamble (or *prèambule*, in French).

OPPOSITE In the centuries after his death, Montagnard leader Robespierre has been alternately viewed by historians as a lunatic and as a more complex figure.

an exceedingly violent one. Some historians suggest that the French Revolution was able to reach such heights of extreme violence because of political leaders such as Robespierre who fanned the flames of discontent with their persuasive and suggestive speeches.

"If virtue be the spring of a popular government in times of peace, the spring of that government during a revolution is virtue combined with terror: virtue, without which terror is destructive; terror, without which virtue is impotent [helpless]. Terror is only justice prompt, severe and inflexible; it is then an emanation [a product] of virtue; it is less a distinct principle than a natural consequence of the general principle of democracy, applied to the most pressing wants of the country."

Maximilien Robespierre, Montagnard leader during the Reign of Terror, 1794

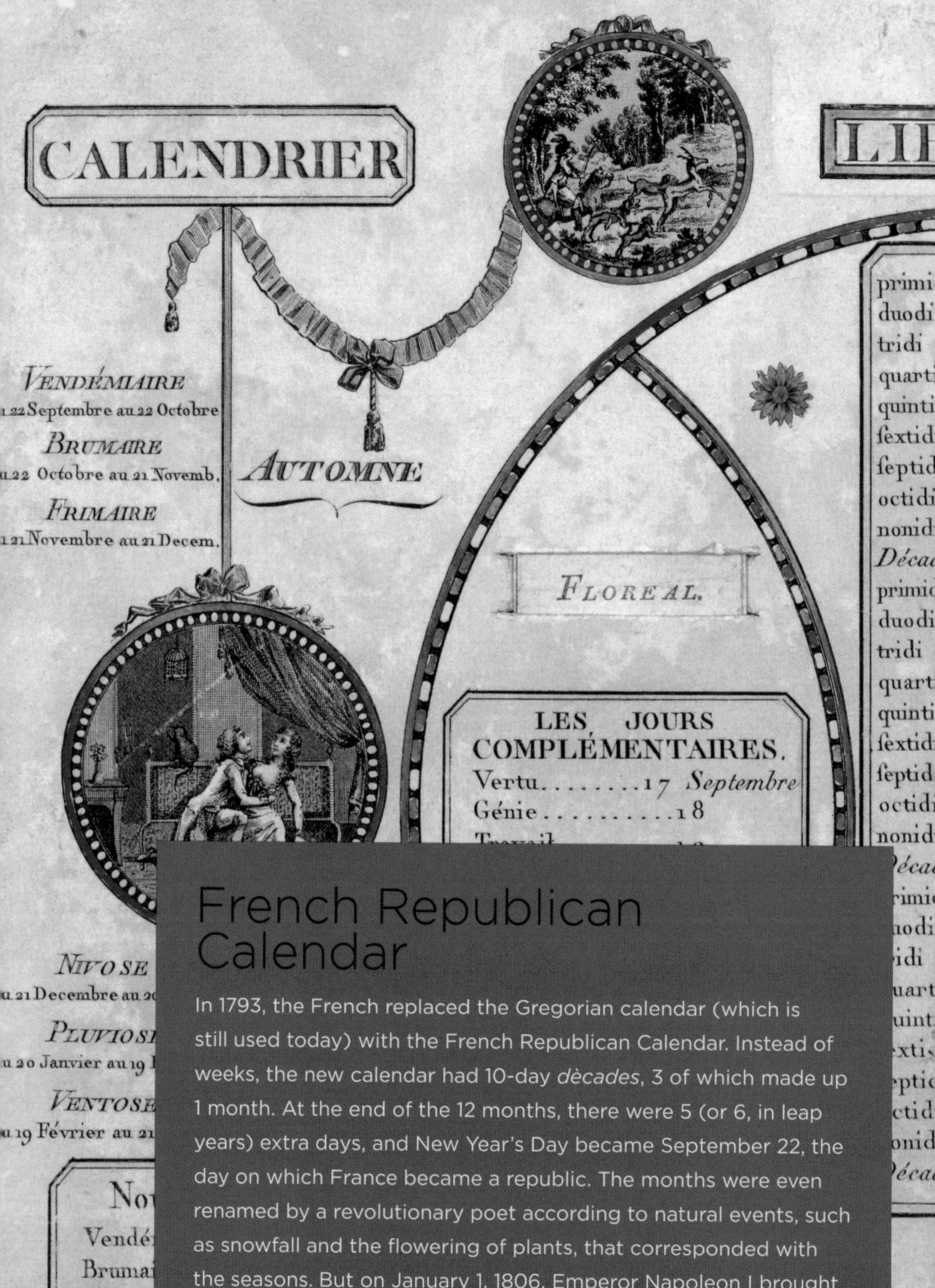

French Republican Calendar

In 1793, the French replaced the Gregorian calendar (which is still used today) with the French Republican Calendar. Instead of weeks, the new calendar had 10-day *dècades*, 3 of which made up 1 month. At the end of the 12 months, there were 5 (or 6, in leap years) extra days, and New Year's Day became September 22, the day on which France became a republic. The months were even renamed by a revolutionary poet according to natural events, such as snowfall and the flowering of plants, that corresponded with the seasons. But on January 1, 1806, Emperor Napoleon I brought back the Gregorian calendar.

TE
PERPÉTUEL.
PRINTEMS
GERMINAL
du 21 Mars au 20 Avril.
FLORÉAL
du 20 Avril au 20 Mai.
PRAIRIAL
du 20 Mai au 19 Juin.
JUIN
Dimanche 1 8 15 22 29
Lundi 2 9 16 23 30
Mardi 3 10 17 24 31
Mercredi 4 11 18 25
Jeudi 5 12 19 26
Vendredi 6 13 20 27
Samedi 7 14 21 28
AN 1801
ÉTÉ
MESSIDOR
du 19 Juin au 19 Juillet.
THERMIDOR
du 19 Juillet au 18 Aout
FRUCTIDOR
du 18 Aout y compris le 16 Sep.
Vieux style.
Janvier...31 Juillet....31
Février...28 Aout.....31
Mars.....31 Septemb..30
Avril....30 Octobre..31
Mai......31 Novemb...30
Juin.....30 Décemb...31
9 Thermidor An 2
où 27 Juillet 1794

OPPOSITE Today, the celebration of Bastille Day usually begins with a grand parade along the Champs-Èlysées and concludes with fireworks over the Eiffel Tower in Paris.

Ordinary citizens would have to have been pushed over the edge to act the way they did. Others would argue that the events of the Revolution were the inevitable result of an explosive combination of callous government, economic crises, and friction between the classes.

Had the Revolution never occurred, though, France would have been a vastly different country. One clear beneficial outcome of the Revolution was that it gave France the opportunity to learn how to handle representation in government (using such bodies as the Estates-General and

National Assembly). It also provided the country with the experience of having branches of government that would serve to check each other's power. These, of course, were incomplete and failed experiments at first, quickly snuffed out by the driving force of Bonaparte, but later, the French would build on the principles with greater success and establish a lasting republic in the mid-20th century.

Since 1880, Bastille Day (July 14) has been celebrated in France and other parts of the world as an official holiday. Marked by parades, speeches, fireworks, and parties, the day honors the anniversary of one of the most critical turning points in French history. Out of a day of violence and bloodshed has come a day of celebration. Out of a time of turmoil and unrest has come a country of great strength, one that is determined to not allow the sacrifices of its revolutionary ancestors to have been in vain.

Bibliography

Andress, David. *The Terror: The Merciless War for Freedom in Revolutionary France*. New York: Farrar, Straus and Giroux, 2005.

Burton, Richard. *Blood in the City: Violence and Revelation in Paris, 1789–1945*. Ithaca, N.Y.: Cornell University Press, 2001.

Doyle, William. *Origins of the French Revolution*. Oxford: Oxford University Press, 1980.

Godechot, Jacques. *The Taking of the Bastille: July 14th, 1789*. Translated by Jean Stewart. New York: Scribner's, 1970.

Melzer, Sara E., and Leslie W. Rabine, eds. *Rebel Daughters: Women and the French Revolution*. New York: Oxford University Press, 1992.

Schama, Simon. *Citizens*. New York: Knopf, 1989.

Solé, Jacques. *Questions of the French Revolution: A Historical Overview*. Translated by Shelley Temchin. New York: Pantheon Books, 1989.

Index